Unselfish Patriotism.

A SERMON

PREACHED IN ST. JOHN'S CHURCH, DETROIT,

ON THE EVENING OF SEXAGESIMA SUNDAY,

FEBRUARY 23, 1862,

BY THE RECTOR,

THE REV. WILLIAM E. ARMITAGE.

DETROIT:
PUBLISHED BY RICHMONDS & BACKUS.
O. S. GULLEY'S STEAM PRESSES.
1862.

This Sermon is printed, at the request of some who heard it, who have so urged the possibility of its helping the good cause a little, that the writer could not well refuse to listen to the motives and the hope with which it was preached, in the ordinary course of his duties.

SERMON.

"Seekest thou great things for thyself? Seek them not."—JEREMIAH 45:5.

THOSE were dark days in which Baruch, the son of Neriah, received this word from the Lord by the mouth of Jeremiah the prophet. It was the fifth year of Jehoiakim, king of Judah, who had come to the throne as the vassal of the king of Egypt, when the land was but the battle-ground of the Egyptians and Chaldeans. The people were divided. Having lost their independence, they could not agree in the choice of masters, and therefore were preyed upon by their powerful neighbors in turn. Amid all the miseries from these causes, the few servants of the LORD among them were grieved and wearied by the general apostasy. They saw the LORD's hand in the judgments which had come upon them; and they believed that the LORD would deliver them, if the blended people could be brought to turn to Him again. With what hope must Jeremiah have heard the command to "write in the roll of a book all the words that had been spoken against Israel, and against Judah, and against all the nations;" when it was added, "it may be that the house of Judah will hear all the evil which I purpose to do unto them; that they may return every man from his evil way; that I may forgive their iniquity and their sin." With what alacrity did he call Baruch, his scribe, to write from his mouth all that the LORD had spoken, and send him to read it in the ears of all the people. On a fast day, when the Temple was thronged, Baruch stood at the entry of the new gate, and read the roll. He was called to read it the second time before all the princes, who seemed to be moved by it. But knowing the king's temper, they counseled him and his master to hide themselves, before he received it at their hands. And it was well that they were hidden, for Jehoiakim, as the roll was read to him, cut off piece after piece and cast it into the fire that was on the hearth; and when it was all consumed, commanded his officers to "take Baruch the scribe, and Jeremiah the prophet," designing instant revenge.

And now in this danger and confinement the characters of the two men were disclosed. Both stood in the same condemnation, to the king; both were servants of GOD; both grieved over the nation's apostasy, and prayed for revival and deliverance; both had expected much, or rather had hoped for much, from the reading of the roll; and now both were disappointed. But while Jeremiah was patient, and willing to suffer for the cause of GOD and his country, since that was required of him, Baruch was crying "Woe is me now! for the LORD hath added grief to my sorrow; I fainted in my sighing, and I find no rest." It was not from difference of natural temperament merely; but while Jeremiah forgot himself, had worked and hoped for GOD and his country, and not for himself, Baruch had been seeking for himself great things. He had been ready enough to write and to read the roll; eager in looking forward to the revival which it seemed to promise; but he had never lost sight of himself in it all. He had hoped to play some chief part, to better his own fortunes. And so the disappointment, which his master felt as a patriot and a servant of GOD, was to him personal and selfish. Jeremiah had the comfort that such was the LORD's will, and he could bear patiently. Baruch fretted and pined, because there was no comfort in expecting great things, and then being forced to hide himself to save his life. The LORD's message to him was, in effect, While thy country is in ruin, seekest thou great things for thyself? Seek them not. I will bring evil upon all flesh. In the coming days great things will be nothing worth. I will give thee thy life in all places whither thou goest, and thou shall often have cause for joy that even so much is sure to thee.

Are not our days, my brethren, like that fifth year of Jehoiakim, king of Judah? Days of national distress, in which national existence is in peril? Worse than foreign invasion is the domestic treason which has brought us into civil war; and I do not know that the miseries of that ancient people were more or greater than our own, past and present and to come. And many a righteous soul among us must have some degree of Jeremiah's feeling for our country. I suppose that, then, the Chaldean and Egyptian parties in Jerusalem were busy in mutual recriminations, exposures, denunciations, tracing to one another all the common woes, and using falsehood when truth would not serve the turn. But Jeremiah went below all such causes to their root in the people's forgetfulness of GOD. All his efforts and prayers, as well as his inspired acts and words, were aimed at arousing them to their peril from that cause. It grieved him, it vexed his soul, that the nation's conscience was dead, and that the LORD's offers were spurned or unheeded. And this should be the Christian patriot's attitude now in this country. Every man who believes in GOD and loves his country, for that country's sake should be a better servant of GOD than he has ever been. It is a cheap and easy patriotism to *talk*; it is a time for every one to *do*. And no man, woman, or child, is without opportunity of doing, if we will keep the prophet's example in mind. Whoever is called to serve in the field, or in any sphere of administration, let him do it heartily, as to the Lord and not to men; seeking, by Christian fidelity, to gain God's blessing on the work. If no such charge is laid upon us, we may find something to do at home for the good cause, perhaps in the care of our soldiers or their families. But, whatever it be, let it be done, not grudgingly, or of necessity, for God loveth a cheerful giver to country as well as to Himself. But, if we can do nothing else, we can give to our cause the help of prayers and efforts for holy living. Every man who adds himself to the number of daily intercessors with God for the removal of His judgments from us; of those whose conscientious living lessens so much the general corruption, wins back so much of the Divine favor; of those who feel with their whole souls that all our evils flow from forgetfulness of God, and so look beyond all means and policy to that return and zeal which should control means and policy—every man who adds himself to the number of real, living, working, praying, consistent Christians, and does all he can to make ours a Christian land, is therein a patriot. Who, do you think, did the most for Judah, in the days of Jeremiah? Who was doing the most, when Baruch and he lay hidden? You heard in the first lesson to-night, (Jeremiah 36 : 11, 12,) the names of the princes and great men of the time. You can conceive of their efforts to save the country—but was not the hidden prophet, day by day appealing to the Lord, interceding, imploring, confessing, accomplishing more than they all? We *must* learn, my brethren, to see God in our history; the forsaking of God in our corruptions; the punishment of God in our fearful war; the need of return to God, of the awakening of the nation's conscience towards God, as the sole hope of peace and lasting union. And, therefore, we ought all to be zealous in these times, for the increase of the Saviour's confessed disciples among us. Besides all other pleaders, your country now takes up the Gospel call to the life of repentance and faith. She cries to every one of us, Be a Christian in all earnestness of heart and soul, and though you be hidden from the public eye, you may have power with God, and do for me more than many a man whose name is ringing through the land. Would to God, that these days were writing in His book, the names of some of us, as helpers of our country, wielding the prophet's sacred and powerful weapons!

Such, beloved, is the lesson of Jeremiah's patriotism. And now we must notice that flaw in his companion, which forbids us to join them in the same praise. Baruch may have shared his master's convictions, and even his prayers and intercessions; but all the while he was seeking great things for himself. He hoped much, and desired much for his country, but no less that return of her prosperity would bear himself to honors. I am afraid that there are more Baruchs than Jeremiahs among us now. When the war began, the first enthusiasm called forth many instances of real self-sacrificing patriotism; which was content to leave home and fair prospects, and serve in the ranks, not even pausing to ask for office. And there has been more of this good spirit, I think, among the privates of our army, than among the officers, whose self-seeking, in too many instances, has done great harm by putting unfit men in posts of responsibility. Seeking great things for themselves, they have found very small things for themselves and their country. Presumptuous ambition carried them straight on to failure and contempt.

But time, and military discipline, will correct these evils in our army, in a measure at least; but let us ask of God that He will mercifully avert from our loved ones in the field all evil consequences from the incapacity, still unexposed.

But leaving the Baruchs of the army, let us look at those nearer home. We have had to bear the reproach of a people greedy of gain; and though some of those casting this stone live in very brittle houses, we have had to confess that the reproach was deserved. The only "great thing" we seem to have cared for has been wealth, every other prize, even public office and power, being no more than a means to obtain it. We knew all this, but we could hardly have realized the thorough possession of us by this evil spirit, until the war revealed it. We had learned to laugh about patriotism, and the fourth of July, and so on, which was a bad sign for us. But, I think, that we would have expected that the danger of the overthrow of our union and constitution, would have disclosed real patriotism, and set self-sacrifice for its sake very generally in the place of the greed of gain. The worst revelation of the war, the proof and the worst symptom of our corruption, has been, that our danger has done no such thing. On the other hand, the war has been almost welcomed as a golden opportunity of gain. Business prospects were rather dull at first, except to the few who were placed in sight of immediate profits from the government's necessities. But as those became more definite, and more public, the clouds lifted. The many saw avenues to profit opening before them, and rushed, at once, to secure their chances. Within the limits of integrity, we have no fault to find with this eagerness of trade. It was legitimate and right, that the war should do us all possible good, to atone somewhat for its far surpassing evils. But O where was the love of country among us? What had become of honor, of integrity, of common honesty, when the greed of gain could drive American citizens to cheat, and plunder, and lie, as we have heard from day to day? What treachery, what inhumanity, what depravity, what willingness for even murder, must fraud and selfishness hide within them—if they would strip our soldiers to the winter by clothing them in rotten fabrics; if they would send our troops to dangerous coasts in vessels condemned for the navigation of quiet rivers; if they would put stores of water, on which many lives depend, in casks which would ruin it for use; if in arms, in ammunition, in means of transport, in horses, in food, in clothing, in everything which our army touches or needs, they would sacrifice comfort, health, life, success, country, all to their paltry gains. It is on record for all future time and for the judgment day, that when our country was in extreme peril, when thousands of her sons rose in her defence, there were found among us men so selfish, so besotted in selfishness, as to seek great things for themselves at the expense of fearful immeasurable injury to hundreds and thousands, and perhaps to our cause. I know not, my brethren, whether any of you have had part in this iniquity. I do not, and cannot suspect you of it. Had I suspected any one of you, as your pastor set here to watch for your souls, I should have implored you, privately, as now publicly, to touch not a single farthing of such ill-gotten gains. They will never profit one hand that has gathered them. Men may hug themselves for their sharpness, and heap up the treasure wrung from their country and her citizens by fraud; but the canker of the LORD's curse is on every coin, and will cling to them in its spending. Better a thousand times be their prey, a wronged and shivering soldier bearing the added hardships of their wickedness, than one of them—rich, if such possessions be riches, but in the Lord's sight thieves and robbers, to be condemned forever, unless with penitence towards Him, they restore the wages of iniquity.

But I did not choose my subject only to add my denunciations of public corruption to those which have been heard from all sides. We have passed beyond Baruch in the scale of self-seeking. He was not so bad as the men we have been compelled to notice. And so, recalling nothing that has been said, lest there may have been some unsuspected need of hearing the truth spoken of the worst offenders, let us consider how near we all are to Baruch's danger in this crisis of our country. He was a patriot, but with the alloy of selfishness; and Judah then needed pure and unselfish patriotism. And this is our need now—unselfish patriotism—the love of our country, in whatever lot of life we are, without seeking great things, or anything, for ourselves. I know how rare disinterestedness is, how almost wild it seems to expect it in these days, but, as a minister of Christ, I must press it upon you, my people, as a need and a duty, whatever be the spirit of the times. You need not follow the multitude; you may be honorable exceptions, if you will. This is no time for men to be seeking great things, when all is in danger which would give value to any of them. Our country should have all our help, of whatever kind; and we are unworthy citizens if we withhold it until we can sell it to her. Your own fortune may not be growing just now; you may feel your business depressed by the war. Well, then, there begins your opportunity for patriotism. Consider it a sacrifice required of you, like Jeremiah's forced concealment, and bear it patiently, as he did. Many are disposed to murmur and grumble; many more to find fault with the administration of affairs; many are keeping up the wretched party-spirit which has brought our woes upon us; but all this should have come to an end long ago. The war is upon us. We cannot help ourselves. To make the best of it, to contribute all we can to unanimity, is surely the wise course. Let us count it unmanly to be selfishly complaining, when we are all suffering as a nation. And this may shield you from the temptation, which may come in this state of dissatisfaction and depression, "to make money out of the government." Now, my brethren, we have admitted that an opportunity of supplying some of the government's necessities may be a legitimate piece of business. But I beseech you, not doubting you, but fearing the power of prevailing sophistries, not to give a shadow of approval to any enterprise, which in the slightest degree takes advantage of the government's necessities. Beware of the lightest influence of the notion, that it is right for you to charge the government more than you dare to charge your fellow-merchants. Some of you may think that I had better let business alone; but it is right for me to urge upon you, now, that the country should be favored instead of overcharged, by her citizens. It is high time that the principle should be established among us, that they should give to the country, instead of making her give to them. The tone of public morals should be elevated, until, wild as the hope may be, men will seek public contracts when they can save for the government, instead of looking on them as fine chances for themselves.

You may urge two thoughts against me. The first is, that, in the present corruption, such patriotic unselfishness will be quite wasted; what you save or give will be thrown away in some other quarter: and the second is, that you may as well have the money as any one else. And it is the prevalence of just such notions, such excuses and palliations, such claims, "that a man can't expect disinterestedness in trade," that "trade is one thing, and fine ideas of morality and virtue another," which seems to require the repetition of the LORD's word to Baruch. If trade be so far from the true standard of right and wrong, then the sooner you leave it the better. But you should not so slander your calling. You are as capable of high-minded, honorable, conscientious dealing, as men of any walk in life. There is no inherent wickedness in trade—no inevitable need of tricks, and sharpness, and selfishness. Whenever you condescend to either, you do wrong to trade as well as to yourselves. Never allege such excuses for violating your own conscience. If your honesty saves, or your patriotism gives to the government a dollar, you shall not lose the reward of honesty and patriotism, if your neighbor robs it of a thousand. And as to its being as well for you to have the money as any one else, do you not blush as you say it? Right and wrong are in your own balance, are right and wrong to you, whatever they may seem to others. Better let all your neighbors get rich, outstrip you in the race, if they can, than let your selfishness wrong your country of a farthing. Seekest thou great things for thyself? Seek them not, saith the LORD. The nearer you can come to forgetfulness of yourself and your own selfish interests, in this crisis of our nation, the nearer you come to true and worthy patriotism. I beseech you, brethren, whatever your opportunities, if they be no more than the cheerful payment of your taxes, to school yourselves to feel that you must now think of your country next to your GOD, and be ready to make sacrifices for her if she demands, or if not, to bear your part of her burden without complaint or selfish murmuring.

There is a beautiful German legend, to borrow the recent illustration of another, on another subject, "that on the return of every spring-time the Emperor Charlemagne comes from his grave to bless the land over which he once held sway; that up and down the Rhine he walks, flinging his blessing on gardens, and vineyards, and fields, to multiply the vintage and the harvest." So, will we hope, may the memory of the Father of his country, whose birth-day was wisely celebrated yesterday, come forth among us on each of these anniversaries and bless us with his great and good example. The almost prophetic wisdom of his Farewell Address, I trust, stirred many hearts yesterday, and recalled them from the tangled paths of our present politics to the sure ground on which our fathers stood. I trust that many eyes, half blinded by prejudices and misunderstandings, were lightened to see the worth of our country, our Union, Constitution, government, as they looked for a while on the services of him who was foremost in their creation. And, above all things, I trust that many minds recalled his unselfish patriotism, of which there is no more illustrious instance. If you would know a man who never needed Baruch's admonition, that man was George Washington. Before his elevation to the head of the army, he wrote to his brother: "It is my full intention to devote my life and fortune in the cause in which we are engaged, if needful." The Congress, when they appointed him Commander-in-Chief, voted him a monthly stipend; but he at once replied, "I beg to assure the Congress, that as no pecuniary consideration could have tempted me to accept this arduous employment, at the expense of my domestic ease and happiness, I do not wish to make any profit from it. I will keep an exact account of my expenses. Those, I doubt not, they will discharge; and that is all I desire." Accordingly, at the close of the war, he gave in the account of his expenditures, and they amounted, in seven years, to ten thousand pounds sterling, "a sum," said a British journal of the time, "which would scarcely have answered the demands of one of our commanders-in-chief a single month." Nor did he show his disinterestedness in money matters only. He was doubted, and censured, and criticised, as the head of our army now is—may God give him strength to stand his ground as well—no idea of escaping from all this ever swerved him a moment. He suffered keenly. A selfish man would have yielded, and refused to suffer longer. Mount Vernon must have had many charms for the commander at Valley Forge; but for his country's sake he bore all that envy, malice, ignorance and rashness brought against him, being sustained by that grace which he daily sought from Heaven, and he has been rewarded by the affection which wonders now that he could ever have been opposed. And then that crowning act of renunciation of great things—his retirement to private life, when he might have grasped the sceptre of power for a lifetime, with the acclamations of a grateful people, has almost drawn the world to say with Lord Erskine, "I feel for him an awful reverence." It was a good thought to make much of his birth-day; and we may hope and pray, that, all over the land, our citizens may have been roused to the difference between the patriotism which seeks for itself, and that like his, knowing no self before country; between the patriotism of Baruch and that of Jeremiah; between the spirit which "thinks only of the best modes in which public calamity can be turned to private gain," and that which will claim no wages, refuse no suffering, for the sacred cause whose success will be recompense enough when shared with the whole rescued people.

"Seekest thou great things for thyself? Seek them not." The precept, my brethren, like all given in God's Word, is of universal application. I have chosen, to-night, to turn it to our country's present claims upon us; and I beg you not to dismiss the subject from your thoughts until you realize your own concern in it, and your ability to be both active and unselfish patriots, whatever your lot in life—active, by prayers and Christian living, if you can do no more; and unselfish, in the cheerful readiness to bear your share of the common burdens, and to help on the good cause even with sacrifices, "if needful." But let me close by commending the principle to you, for your guidance in all relations. It is the very mind of Jesus Christ, the Great Exemplar. The natural heart enthrones self for its deity; and no man can be either good, or wise, or great, until that idol is cast down. Ask yourself, what is the general tenor of your life? Are you living for yourself? Are you seeking great things for yourself? Have you not the habit of considering the claims of God your Saviour, of His Church, of your fellow-men, of your country, of your community upon you? Are you thinking and planning and toiling every day, only for yourself? Then, oh my friend, you know not what life may be. You have never tasted its purest joys. The best part of your soul is undeveloped. Begin, at once, to live for others and for God. Count it unworthy to be selfish and self-seeking. This transitory world is no place for seeking great things, which soon shall surely perish. Seek them not. Seek to make the world better and happier for your living in it. Seek to be like Him who "pleased not Himself;" who spared Himself no toil, no shame, no pang for your redemption. And every act of self-denial, every sacrifice, every generous, unselfish, loving word or deed, shall bring you a reward in His future kingdom from our dear LORD, a thousand fold more precious than all the great things which now allure your seeking.

www.ingramcontent.com/pod-product-compliance
Lightning Source LLC
LaVergne TN
LVHW050339200826
846010LV00032B/345
* 9 7 8 1 4 1 8 1 9 0 1 3 2 *